The Wonderful Universe of

ALLAH

INSPIRING THOUGHTS FROM
THE QUR'ĀN ON NATURE

Presented to ....

From ....

Date ....

The Wonderful Universe of
ALLAH

INSPIRING THOUGHTS FROM
THE QUR'ĀN ON NATURE

COMPILED BY
SANIYASNAIN KHAN

Goodword
B·O·O·K·S

For my mother

• • •

First published 1997
© Goodword Books, 1997

Distributed by
AL-RISALA
The Islamic Centre
1, Nizamuddin West Market, Near DESU, New Delhi 110 013
Tel. 4611128, 4611131 Fax: 91-11-4697333
E-mail: risala. islamic. @ axcess. net. in.

Photographs by
Ruqaiyyah Waris Maqsood, Saniyasnain Khan and Elena Rushbrook

Artwork and typesetting by
K.M. Ravindran, V.K. Kannan, Saji Maramon, Mohd. Nasir and Mohd. Imran

Thanks are due to Mrs. Anna Khanna, Ruqaiyyah Waris Maqsood and
Susan Brady Maitra for their immense help in making this book possible.

Designed and produced by Goodword Press, New Delhi.

Allah's creation is wonderful; His beauty is in everything—every tiny grain of sand, every raindrop, every leaf, rock or stream. Allah's care and handiwork can be sensed in the very air we breathe.

We human beings are part of Allah's creation—a very significant part of it. We are different from all other animals in that we have a highly developed sense of awareness of all manner of things. Other animals are aware of their environments and experience a certain range of basic emotions, but they are not conscious in the way that we are.

Whether or not other animals have souls is part of *al-Ghayb*, i.e. those facts of our universe which have been placed beyond human understanding. But, in the view of all religious people, it is beyond all doubt that human beings have souls—that we are spiritual beings.

We journey through life, abiding in our particular physical setting for only the briefest of moments. However, this setting in which we live—our universe—like the mother's womb in which an unborn child grows and develops is a much more permanent thing. There we undergo all sorts of experiences, observing and drawing conclusions—that is what Allah intended for us.

The created universe is full of Signs to induce people to reflect upon what lies before them. It is not just a random system, that came into being on its own by chance. Every single created thing has Signs in it, from which we can learn.

One of the aspects of human life most frequently commented upon in the Qur'ān is its temporality. It is also mentioned time and again that we will all be created anew for a life in an entirely different dimension at a time when

God wills. Signs for this vary from the changing seasons, with the new growth of vibrant greenery after the seeming death of the land, to the incredible metamorphosis of living things from one stage of existence to another—for example, the wingless insects that lived once as crawling creatures acquiring wings and flying.

Allah lends us this special planet, the Blue Planet Earth, trusting us with its care, and granting us the use of all its treasures. Just as we respect Allah Himself, we must also respect His creation.

We can never number His blessings; full understanding is beyond our grasp. Yet we can love Him, and respond to His blessings in love and gratitude. We can study the things spread out before us and learn from them and draw hope from them. Through a wider appreciation of His wonderful creation, we can praise and honour the Almighty.

RUQAIYYAH WARIS MAQSOOD

HULL (U.K.)

In the creation of the heavens and
the earth and the alternation of night and day
and ships that sail the ocean with profitable cargoes
and the water Allah sends down from the sky
with which He revives the earth after it is dead,
scattering over it all manner of beasts,
and the turning about of the winds
and the clouds driven between heaven and earth—
surely in all these are signs for people who
have sense.

(2:164)

The Kingdom of the heavens
and the earth belongs to God;
and God has power over everything.
Surely in the creation of the heavens and earth
and in the alternation of night and day
there are signs for people who reflect—
who remember God, whether standing, sitting
or lying down, and reflect upon
the creation of the heavens and the earth,
praying:
'Our Lord, You have not created this
for no purpose.
Glory be to You! Keep us safe from the
punishment of the Fire.

(3:190-191)

All the beasts that roam the earth,
and all the creatures that fly on two wings,
are similar communities to your own.
We have left out nothing in the Book;
then to their Lord they shall all be gathered.

(6:38)

$\mathcal{I}$t is Allah who splits the seed
and the fruit-stone.
He brings forth the living from the dead,
and the dead from the living.
Such is Allah; how you can turn away?
He kindles the light of dawn,
and has made the night for rest,
and the sun and moon for measuring (our time).
That is the ordaining of the Almighty,
the All-knowing.
It is He who has created the stars for you,
that they may guide you through the darkness
of land and sea.
We have made plain Our revelations to people
who have sense.
It is He who produced you from one living soul,

and provided you with a dwelling
and a resting-place.
We have made plain Our revelations to people
who reflect carefully.
It is He who sends down water from the sky,
and with it We bring forth the shoots
of every plant.
From these We bring forth green foliage,
and close-growing grain,
palm-trees laden with dates thick-clustered,
ready to the hand, and gardens of vines,
olives, pomegranates, alike and different.
Behold their fruits when they ripen!
Surely, in all this are signs for true believers.

(6:95-99)

$\mathscr{I}$t is He who produces gardens
trellised and untrellised,
palm-trees, and crops of so many different kinds—
olives, pomegranates, alike and different.
Eat of their fruits when they ripen,
and pay the poor due thereof on the harvest day;
and be not prodigal; God loves not the prodigal.

(6:141)

14

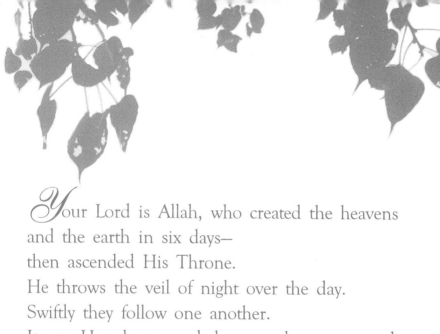

Your Lord is Allah, who created the heavens
and the earth in six days—
then ascended His Throne.
He throws the veil of night over the day.
Swiftly they follow one another.
It was He who created the sun, the moon, and
the stars and made them subservient to His will.
His is the creation, His the command.
Blessed be Allah, the Lord of the Universe.

(7:54)

He sends the winds, bearing good tidings
of His mercy, and when they are charged with
heavy clouds, We drive it on to a dead land
and let the water fall upon it, bringing forth all
manner of fruits.
In the same way will We raise the dead to life:
perchance you will remember.
And the good land—its vegetation comes forth
by the leave of its Lord,
but the barren soil gives a scanty yield.
Thus do We make plain Our revelations to those
who render thanks.

(7:57-58)

16

Will they not ponder upon the kingdom
of the heavens and the earth,
and all that God has created, to see whether
their hour is not drawing near?
And in what other revelation will they believe,
those that deny this?

(7:185)

Your Lord is God, Who created
the heavens and the earth in six days,
then ascended His throne,
ordaining all things. Intercessor
there is none, save by His leave.
Such is God, your Lord; so serve Him.
Will you not take heed?

(10:3)

*I*t was He that gave the sun its shining
brightness
and the moon its reflected radiance,
regulating her phases, so that you
may learn to predict the seasons and the years.
Allah created them only to manifest the Truth.
He makes plain His revelations to people of
understanding.
In the alternation of night and day,
and in all that Allah has created in the heavens
and on the earth, there are signs for
God-fearing people.

(10:6)

Say: 'Who provides for you from heaven and earth?
Who has endowed you with hearing and sight?
Who brings forth the living from the dead and the dead from the living?
Who ordains all things?
They will surely reply, 'God.' Then say: 'Will you not take heed?'

(10:31)

Say: 'Behold what is in the heavens and in the earth!' But neither signs nor warnings will avail a people who do not believe.

(10:101)

19

No creature is there on the earth,
but its sustenance rests on Allah;
He knows its dwelling
and its resting-place.
All is recorded in a glorious book.

(11:6)

God is He who raised up the heavens
without visible pillars,
then He ascended His throne.
He subjected to His will the sun and the moon,
each following His appointed laws.
He ordains all things.
He explains His signs in detail so that you may
believe with certainty in meeting your Lord.
It was He who spread out the earth
and set firm mountains and rivers on it,
and fruit of every kind.
He created in pairs two and two,
and He draws the veil of night over the daylight.
Surely in these things there are signs for people who
reflect. And on the earth are adjoining stretches
of land, and vineyards, and fields of grain,

and palms, single and clustered, (which are)
watered by the same water—
yet some of them We have favoured above others
in excellence of taste.
Surely in that are signs for a people
who understand.

(13:2-4)

It is He who makes the lightning flash
upon you, which can fill you with both fear
and hope; It is He who raises up clouds heavy
with rain. The thunder proclaims His praise,
and the angels, too, in awe of Him.
He looses the thunderbolts, and smites with them
whomsoever He will; yet the unbelievers

dispute about God, and the strength of His power.
His is the true prayer.
Any idols to which the pagans pray
give them no answer.
They are like a man who stretches out his hands
to the water and bids it rise to his mouth,
but it cannot reach there.
The prayers of those without faith are nothing
but futile wanderings.
To Allah shall bow all who are in the heavens
and the earth, willingly, or in spite of themselves,
as do their very shadows in the mornings
and the evenings.
Say: 'Who is the Lord and sustainer
of the heavens and of the earth?'

Say: 'Allah.'

Say: 'Do you then take others besides Him
to be your protectors,
such as have no power to profit or hurt even
themselves?'

Say: 'Are the blind equal with those who see?
Or the depth of darkness equal with light?
Have their idols brought into being a creation
like His, so that both creations appear to
them alike?'

Say: 'Allah is the Creator of everything,
and He is the One, the Omnipotent.'

He sends down water from the skies,
which fills the rivers to overflowing,
so that the torrent bears away the foam that rises
to the surface.

Similarly, there is a scum which rises
from smelted ore when men make
ornaments and tools.
In such a manner does Allah depict the true
and the false.
As for the scum, it vanishes as jetsam,
but that which is useful to humankind remains
behind.
Thus does Allah set forth His parables.

(13:12-17)

Have you not seen how Allah
compares a good word to a good tree?
Its roots are firm,
and its branches are in the sky;
it yields its fruit in every season
by the leave of its Lord.
So Allah speaks in parables to people
so that they may take heed.
But an evil word is like an evil tree—
torn out of the earth,
and shorn of all its roots.
Allah will strengthen the faithful with His
steadfast Word, in the present life
and in the world to come;
Allah leads astray the evildoers;
Allah does what He will.

(14:24–27)

*I*t was Allah who created the heavens
and the earth,
and sent down water from the skies
with which He brought forth food to sustain you.
And He made subject to you the ships
which sail upon the sea at His command;
and He created the rivers for your benefit
as well as the sun and moon,
constant upon their courses.
He has also made subject to you the night
and day,
and given you all you have asked for.
If you counted God's blessings, you could never
number them; surely people are sinful, and
unthankful!

(14:32-34)

*W*e have set out the Signs of the Zodiac
in the heavens and endowed them with beauty
for all to behold, and made them secure
against every accursed satanic force—so that anyone
who seeks to learn (the unknowable) by stealth
is pursued by a flame clear to see.
And the earth—We stretched it out,
and set upon it immovable mountains,
and caused life of every kind to grow on it in a
balanced manner, providing sustenance for you
as well as those for whom you do not provide.
No single thing exists that does not have
its storehouse with Us, and We bestow nothing
from on high unless it be in
appropriate measure.
And We let loose the winds to fertilise (plants) and

We send down out of heaven water
from the skies for you to drink;
its stores are beyond your reach.
We ordain life and death,
We are the Heir of all things.
We know those who lived before you and those
who will come after you.
It is your Lord who shall muster them all.
He is All-wise, All-knowing.

(15:16-25)

*H*e created the heavens and the earth
to manifest the truth;
Exalted be He above any partners they associate
with Him!

He created man from a (mere) sperm-drop;
and yet this same being is an open adversary.
And the cattle—He created them for you;
You derive warmth and food from them
and other benefits; and you find beauty in them,
when you bring them home to rest in the evenings,
and when you drive them out to pasture
in the mornings.
And they bear your loads to (many) a place
that you could not otherwise reach
without great hardship.
Compassionate is your Lord and merciful.
He has given you horses, and mules, and asses,
to ride as well as use for show.
He has created other things beyond your knowledge.

(16:3-8)

31

$\mathscr{I}$t is He who sends down water from the skies.
You drink of it yourself, as does the vegetation
on which you pasture your herds.
By this means He brings forth for you corn, and
olives, and palms, and vines, and all manner of fruit.
Surely in that is a sign for people who reflect.
And He has made the night and day,
and the sun and moon and all the stars
subservient to His command (that they may be
of use) to you.
Surely in that are signs for people who understand.
And that which He has multiplied for you
on the earth in many colours,
Surely in that is a sign for people who celebrate
the praises of Allah in gratitude.
It is He who subjected to you the sea, that you may

eat its fresh fish, and bring up from its depths
ornaments with which to adorn yourselves.
Behold the ships cleaving through its waters.
All this He has created so that you may seek
His bounty, and render thanks to Him.
He set firm mountains upon the earth
lest it should sway with you;
and rivers, roads and landmarks,
so that you may find your way.
By the stars too, people are guided.
Is He then, who has created, like him
who can not create?
Will you not take heed? If you count God's
blessings, you will never number them.
God is All-forgiving, All-compassionate.

(16:10-18)

$\mathcal{D}$o they not see how all things that Allah has
created cast their shadows to the right and
to the left,
bowing themselves before Him in all humility?
To Allah bow all the creatures of the heavens,
the earth, and the angels too.
They are not arrogant;
they fear their Lord above them,
and do as they are commanded.

(16:48–50)

And it is Allah who sends down water
from the sky, and revives the earth after it is dead.
Surely in that is a sign for a people who have ears.
And in the cattle, too, there is a lesson for you;
We give you to drink of what is within their bellies,
between that which is to be eliminated
and its life-blood—pure milk,
sweet to those who drink it.
And from the fruits of the palms and the vines,
you derive intoxicants as well as wholesome food.

Surely in this is a message for men
of understanding.
And your Lord has inspired the bees, saying:
'Make your homes in the mountains,
in the trees, and in the hives
which people shall build for you.
Then feed on all manner of fruit, and follow humbly
the paths ordained for you by your Lord.'
Then issues forth from their bellies a fluid of
many hues, wherein there is healing for people.
Surely in this is a sign
for people who reflect.

(16:65–69)

To Allah belongs the knowledge of the
Unseen, in the heavens and in the earth.
The business of the Final Hour
shall be accomplished in the twinkling of an eye,
or even in a shorter time.
Allah has power over all things.
And Allah has brought you forth,
knowing nothing, from your mothers' wombs,
and He has given you hearing, and sight,
and hearts, so that you would be thankful.
Do you not see the birds up in the sky
held poised in the air?
None sustains them but Allah; surely in that are
signs for believers. And it is Allah who has given
you houses to dwell in, and has made tents
for you out of the skins of cattle

which you find light and easy to pitch
on the day you travel, and then halt for shelter.
From their wool, fur, and hair He has provided
you with comforts and domestic goods to serve
you for some time. And it is Allah who has given
you shelter from the sun by means of the things
He created; He has given you refuge
in the mountains and He has furnished you
with garments to protect you from the heat,
and coats of armour to protect you in your wars.
Thus He perfects His blessings upon you, so that
you may submit to Him. But if they turn their backs,
your mission is only to give plain warning.
They recognize the blessing of Allah, yet they deny
it. Most of them are ungrateful.

(16:77-83)

*E*at the good and lawful things which Allah has provided you with,
and be thankful for the blessings of Allah,
if you truly serve Him.
These things only He has forbidden you:
carrion, blood, the flesh of swine;
also any flesh consecrated other than in the name of Allah. But whoever is forced (to eat forbidden things) by necessity, desiring neither to sin nor to transgress, will find that Allah is All-forgiving, All-compassionate. Do not falsely declare: 'This is lawful, and that is forbidden,' in order to invent a falsehood about Allah; surely those who invent falsehoods about Allah shall never prosper.

(16:114-116)

We made the night and the day twin marvels.
We enshrouded the night with darkness
and gave light to the day,
so that you might seek the bounty of your Lord
and learn to use the seasons
and the years to make calculations.
We have made all things manifestly plain to you.

(17:12)

Your Lord gives abundantly to whom He will
and sparingly to whom He pleases;
He knows and observes His servants.
Do not kill your children for fear of poverty;
We will provide for you and them;
to kill them is a grievous sin.

(17:30-35)

41

The seven heavens, the earth,
and all who dwell in them extol Him;
all creatures celebrate His praises,
but you do not understand their extolling.
He is All-clement, All-forgiving.

(17:44)

Your Lord it is who drives your ships across
the sea, so that you may sail in them to seek
His bounty;
He is All-compassionate towards you.
When at sea a misfortune befalls you,
all those to whom you pray will forsake you
except Him.
Yet when He brings you safe to dry land,

you turn away; truly, man is ever thankless.
Do you feel confident that He will not
cause the shore to swallow you up,
or let loose against you a deadly sandstorm?
You would find none to protect you.
Are you confident that when you put to sea
again, He will not smite you with a violent
hurricane and drown you for your thanklessness?
Then, you would find none to help you.
We have honoured the Children of Adam
and guided them on land and sea,
and provided them with good things,
and exalted them above many
of Our creatures.

(17:66-70)

Give them this parable.
Once there were two men; to one of them
We granted two vineyards set about with palm-trees,
and watered by a running stream with a cornfield
lying in between.
Each of the two gardens yielded an abundant crop;
so when their owner had gathered in the harvest,
he said to his companion, in the course
of conversation. 'I have a greater abundance of
wealth than you,
and my clan is mightier than yours.'
And as he entered his garden, having thus
wronged his soul, he said, 'I do not think
that this will ever perish! I do not think
that the Hour of Doom will ever come, or that
if I am indeed returned to my Lord,

I will find a better resort than this.'
His companion, continuing the conversation,
replied: 'What makes you disbelieve Him
who created you from dust, from a sperm-drop,
then shaped you as a human being?
As for myself, Allah is my Lord,
and I will not associate anyone with Him.
When you entered your garden,
why did you not say, "Allah's will be done!
There is no power except in Allah"?
Though you see me poorer than yourself
and blessed with fewer children, yet it may be
that my Lord will give me a better garden
than yours, and loose a thunderbolt out of heaven
on your vineyard,
turning it into a barren waste,

or drain its water deep into the earth so that you
will find none of it.'
His fruits were all destroyed,
and in the morning he wrung his hands with
grief at all that he had spent upon them, for the
vines had fallen down upon their trellises, and
he cried:
'Would that I had not served deities other than
my Lord!'
But there was no one to help him,
apart from Allah, and he was helpless.
In such ordeals, protection comes only from
God, the true God. His is the best reward,
and His the best requital.

(18:32-44)

Give them a simile about this life.
It is like the vegetation of the earth
that thrives when watered by the rain
sent down from the skies,
but soon turns into stubble which the winds
scatter.
Allah has power over all things.

(18:45)

Say: 'If the sea were ink with which to write
the words of my Lord,
the sea would surely dry up before the words of
my Lord were exhausted,
though We were to add to it sea upon sea.'

(18:109)

And We set upon the earth firm
mountains
lest it should shake with them,
and We set in it broad paths to serve as
highways,
so that they might find their way,
and We set up the sky as a well-secured canopy;
yet still from Our signs they turn away.
It was He who created the night and the day,
the sun and the moon;
each moving swiftly in its own orbit.

(21:30-33)

And tell of David and Solomon: how they
passed judgement regarding the cornfield in
which strayed lambs had grazed by night.
We gave Solomon insight into the case and bore
witness to both their judgements. We caused the
mountains and the birds to join with David in
Our praise. All this We have done. And We
taught him the armourer's craft, so that you
might have protection in your wars; then are you
thankful? And to Solomon We subjected the
raging wind that sped at his command
to the land that We had blessed;
and We have knowledge of all things;

(21:79-81)

If you are in doubt as to the Resurrection,
remember that We first created you from dust
then from a living germ, then from a blood clot,
then from a half-formed lump of flesh,
so that We might make manifest to you Our power.
And We establish in the wombs
what We will, for an appointed term, then We
deliver you as infants, that you may come of age.
Some of you die young,
and some of you live on to abject old age,
when all that you once knew you know no more.
You sometimes see the earth dry and barren:
but then, when We send down rain upon it,
it begins to stir, and swell, and puts forth
every kind of radiant bloom.

That is because God is Truth:
He brings the dead to life, and has power
over all things.

(22:5-6)

*H*ave you not seen how all who are
in the heavens and all who are in the earth,
the sun and the moon, the stars and
the mountains, the trees and the beasts,
and countless people bow to God?
Yet many have deserved His scourge.
He who is humbled by God
has none to honour him.
God does whatsoever He will.

(22:18)

Thus shall it be. God causes the night to pass
into day and the day into night;
God is All-hearing, All-seeing.
Thus shall it be. God is Truth,
and Falsehood all that they invoke besides Him.
God is the Most High, the Supreme One.
Have you not seen how God has sent
water down out of heaven,
and forthwith the earth becomes green?
Gracious is God and All-Knowing.
To Him belongs all that is in the heavens
and in the earth;
God is the Self-Sufficient, the Glorious One.
Have you not seen how God has subjected
to you all that is in the earth?

He has given you ships which sail the sea
at His command.
He holds the sky lest it should fall upon the earth.
This it shall not do, save by His leave.
Compassionate is God and merciful to mankind.
It is He who gave you life,
who will cause you to die
and who will give you life again.
Surely humanity is ungrateful.

(22:61-66)

$\mathcal{O}$ people, here is a parable set forth!
Listen to it!
Those whom you invoke apart from Allah, could
never create a single fly,
though they all combined together to do it;
and if a fly carried away a speck of dust from
them, they could never retrieve it.
Feeble indeed are those who petition and
those whom they petition.
No just estimate have they made of Allah,
for Allah is All-powerful, Almighty.

(22:73-74)

We first created man from an essence of clay,
then placed him, a living germ,
in a safe enclosure (the womb).
Then We created from the drop a clot;
then We created from the clot a tissue;
then We created from the tissue bones;

then We clothed the bones in flesh,
thus bringing forth another creation.
Blessed be Allah, the noblest of creators!
You shall surely die hereafter,
then on the Day of Resurrection
be restored to life.
We created above you seven heavens,
and We are never heedless of Our creation.

(23:13-17)

We sent down from the skies water
in due measure, and caused it to soak into the soil.
But if We pleased, We could take it all away.
Then with this We produced for you
palm groves and vineyards
in which there are many fruits for your sustenance.
Also a tree growing on Mount Sinai,
which gives oil and a condiment for men.
And surely in the cattle there is an example of
Our power.
You drink of that which is in their bellies, you
eat their flesh, and gain other benefits from
them besides.
By them, as by the ships that sail the sea,
you are carried.

(23:18-22)

It was He who gave you hearing,
and eyes, and hearts;
Yet you are seldom thankful.
It was He who scattered you on the earth,
and before Him you shall all be assembled.
It is He who ordains life, and death,
and He who alternates the night with the day;
can you not understand?

(23:78-80)

Did you think that We had created you for no
reason, and that you would never be recalled to Us?
Exalted be God, the True King!
There is no deity save Him,
the Lord of the noble throne.

(23:115-116)

God is the Light of the heavens and the earth;
His Light may be compared to a niche
wherein is a lamp (the lamp in a glass,
the glass as it were a glittering star)
kindled from a Blessed Tree,
an olive that is neither of the East nor of the West
whose very oil would shine, even if no fire
touched it; Light upon Light;
Allah guides to His Light whom He will.
Allah speaks in metaphors to people.
Allah has knowledge of all things.
His light is found in the houses of worship
which He has allowed to be raised up,
for His Name to be commemorated therein;
glorifying Him, in the mornings and
the evenings,

are people whom neither commerce nor trade
can divert from their remembrance of Allah
or the performance of the prayer, or the giving
of alms,
or the fearing of a day when hearts and eyes
shall writhe with anguish;
who hope that Allah will recompense them for
their noblest deeds
and lavish His grace upon them.
Allah gives without measure to whom He will.

(24:35-38)

$\mathcal{D}$o you not see how Allah
is praised by those in heaven
and those on earth,
even by the birds as they
spread out their wings?
He notes the prayers
and praises of all His creatures,
and has knowledge of all their actions.

(24:41)

To Allah belongs the Kingdom of the heavens
and the earth, and to Him shall all things return.
Have you not seen how Allah drives the clouds,
then gathers and piles them up in masses,
which pour down torrents of rain?
And He sends down out of heaven's mountains,
the hail, smiting whom He will with it, and
turning it aside from whom He will;
The flash of His lightning almost snatches away
human sight.
Allah makes the night succeed the day;
surely in that is a lesson for those who have eyes.
Allah has created every beast from water.
Some go upon their bellies,

others walk upon two feet,
and others yet upon four;
Allah creates whatever He will;
Allah has power over all things.

(24:42–45)

$\mathcal{D}$o you not see how your Lord lengthens
the shadows?
Had it been His will,
He could have made them constant.
But then, We have made the sun their guide;
little by little we shorten them.
It is He who made the night a mantle for you
and sleep a rest.
He makes each day a resurrection.
It is He who has loosed the winds,
bearing good tidings of His mercy;
and We sent down from heaven pure water
so that We might revive the dead land,
and quench the thirst of the countless beasts and
human beings We created.
We have indeed made it flow freely

amongst them,
so that they may remember;
yet most people decline to render thanks.

(25:45-50)

*I*t was He who let forth the two seas,
the one sweet and fresh,
the other salt, and bitter,
and set between them a rampart,
an insurmountable barrier.
It was He who created from
water a mortal, and gave him
kindred of blood and marriage;
All-powerful is your Lord.

(25:53-54)

$\mathscr{P}$ut your trust in the Living God,
who never dies.
Celebrate His praise.
He is well aware of all His servants' sins.
He created the heavens and the earth,
and all that lies between them, in six days,
and then ascended His Throne.
He is the Lord of Mercy: ask those who know of
Him!

(25:58-59)

*B*lessed be He
who has decked the heavens with constellations,
and set among them a lamp (sun),
and an illuminating moon.
And it is He who makes the night succeed the day:
a sign to those who would take heed
and render thanks.

(25:61-62)

*D*o they not see the earth,
how We have brought forth from it all kinds of
beneficial plants?
Surely in that is a sign;
yet most of them do not believe.
Your Lord is the Almighty, the All-compassionate.

(26:7-9)

He who created the heavens and earth,
sent down for you water from the sky;
and We caused to grow therewith gardens full
of delight.
Try as you may, you cannot cause such trees to grow.
Could there be a divine power besides God?
Nay, but they are a people who assign to Him equals!
He who made the earth a firm place
and watered it with flowing rivers
and set upon it immovable mountains
and placed a barrier between the two seas.
Could there be a divine power besides God?
Indeed, most of them have no knowledge.
Surely worthier is He who answers the oppressed,
when they cry out to Him,
and relieves their affliction. It is He who has

appointed you to inherit the earth.
Could there be a divine power besides God?
Little indeed do you reflect!
Worthier is He who guides you in the darkness
of the land and the sea and looses the winds,
bearing good tidings of His mercy.
Could there be a divine power besides God?
Exalted be God, above their idols!
Surely worthier is He Who originates creation,
then brings His creatures back to life hereafter
and gives you sustenance from heaven and earth.
Could there be a divine power besides God?
Say: 'Produce your proof, if you speak truly!'
Say: 'No one knows the Unseen in the heavens
and earth except God!'

(27:60-65)

Have they not seen how We made the night
for them to repose in and the day to give them light?
Surely in that is a sign for a people
who are true believers.

(27:86)

Say: 'Think!' If Allah should enshroud you in perpetual night, until the Day of Resurrection, which deity other than Allah could bring you illumination?

Will you not hear? Say: 'Think! If Allah should give you perpetual day until the Day of Resurrection, which deity other than Allah could bring you night to rest in? Will you not see?'

Of His mercy He has appointed the night for you so that you may rest in it, and the day so that you may seek His bounty, and give thanks.

(28:71-73)

*H*ave they not seen how Allah originates
Creation, then renews it?
Surely that is an easy matter for Allah.
Say: 'Roam the earth, then see how
He originated Creation;
then Allah will initiate the Second Creation;
Allah has power
over all things.'

(29:19-20)

*Y*ou that are true believes among My servants,
My earth is vast; therefore serve Me!

(29:56)

Countless are the beasts that cannot fend for themselves.

God provides for them as He provides for you.

He is the All-Hearer, the All-Knower.

If you ask them

'Who created the heavens and the earth

and subjected the sun and the moon?'

they will say, 'God.'

How then can they turn away from Him?

God grants His sustenance in abundance,

or gives it in scant measure to whomsoever He

will of His servants;

God has knowledge of everything.

If you ask them,

'Who sends down water from the sky, and

therewith revives the earth after it is dead?'
they will say, 'God.'
Say: 'Praise then be to God.'
But most of them have no understanding.
This present life is just a sport and a pastime.
The Last Abode is the true Life,
if they but knew it.
When they set sail in ships,
they call on God, with all fervour;
but when He has delivered them to the land,
they pray to others besides Him,
showing ingratitude for what We have given them,
and giving themselves up to worldly enjoyment;
they will soon know!

(29:60–66)

Allah originates creation, then
He reproduces it.
To Him you shall be recalled.

(30:11)

By one of His signs
He created you from dust; then behold,
you became people, and multiplied throughout
the earth.
By another of His signs He created for you
spouses, from among yourselves,
that you might live in peace with them,
and He has planted love and mercy in your hearts.
Surely in that are signs for people who reflect.

Among His other signs are the creation of the
heavens and earth
and the variety of your languages and colours.
Surely in that are signs for all living beings.
By another of His signs
you slumber by night and seek His bounty by day.
Surely in that are signs for people who hear.
By another of His signs
He shows you lightning, inspiring you with fear
and hope.
He sends down from the sky water
and with it He revives the earth after it is dead.
Surely in that are signs for people who understand.
By another of His signs
heaven and earth stand firm

at His command; when He summons you
by a single call out of the earth,
you shall go forth to Him.
To Him belongs whosoever is in the heavens
and the earth;
all obey His will.
It is He who originates creation,
then renews it.
That is very easy for Him.
His is the most exalted attribute in the heavens
and the earth;
He is the Almighty, the All-wise.

(30:23–27)

*E*vil has become rife on land and sea in
consequence of people's misdeeds.
He has ordained it thus so that people may taste
the fruits of their actions and mend their ways.

(30:41)

*B*y another of His signs
He looses the winds, bearing good tidings
so that you may rejoice in His mercy,
and your ships may sail at His commandment,
and so that you may seek His bounty and be
thankful. Indeed, We sent before you Messengers
to other peoples, and they brought them veritable
signs; then We took vengeance upon those who

sinned; and it was ever a duty incumbent upon Us to help the believers. God is He that looses the winds, that stir up clouds, and He spreads them in heaven as He will, and breaks them up, so that you can see the rain falling from their midst. When He sends it down upon His servants they rejoice, although before its coming they had been in despair.
So behold the marks of God's mercy,
how He quickens the earth after it was dead;
surely it is He who will resurrect the dead.
He has power over all things.
Yet, if We let loose on them a searing wind,
they would return to unbelief.

(30:46-51)

He created the sky without visible pillars,
and He set on the earth firm mountains,
lest it should shake with you. He scattered
abroad in it all manner of beasts,
and sent down water out of the skies,
and caused to grow in it all kinds of goodly plants.
Such is Allah's creation; now show Me anything
that others than He may have created!
Truly, the evildoers are in manifest error.

(31:10-11)

Have you not seen how
Allah has subjected to you whatsoever
is in the heavens and earth,
and lavished on you His blessings,
both seen and unseen?
Yet some still argue about Allah,
without knowledge or guidance, or an
illuminating Book.

(31:20)

*I*f all the trees of the earth were pens,
and the sea were ink, with seven more seas to
replenish it,
the Words of God would still not be exhausted.
God is Almighty, All-wise.

(31:27)

*D*o you not see how God makes the night
pass into the day
and the day into the night?
He has subjected the sun and the moon,
each of them running its course for an
appointed term.
God is aware of all that you do.
That is because God is the Truth, and false are

the idols they invoke besides Him.
God is the Most-high, the Supreme One.
Do you not see how the ships speed upon the
sea by the blessing of God,
so that He may show you some of His signs?
Surely in that are signs for every steadfast,
thankful person.
When the waves envelop them like giant shadows,
they call upon God, in utter devotion.
But no sooner does He bring them safe to land
than some of them falter between faith and
unbelief.
None will deny Our signs,
except the treacherous and the ungrateful.

(31:29-32)

*A*llah alone has knowledge of the Hour of Doom.
He sends down the abundant rain;
He knows what every womb contains.
No mortal knows what he will earn tomorrow,
and no mortal knows in what land he will die.
Allah alone is Wise and All-knowing.

(31:34)

*G*od is He that created the heavens and the earth,
and what between them is, in six days,
then ascended His Throne.
Apart from Him, you have neither protector
nor mediator; will you not take heed?
He governs all, from heaven to earth.
All will ascend to Him in a single day,
a day whose measure is a thousand years by
your reckoning.
He knows the Unseen and the Visible.
He is the All-mighty, the All-compassionate,
who has excelled in the creation of all things.
He first created humanity out of clay,
then fashioned his progeny from a drop of
humble fluid.

Then He shaped him, and breathed His spirit
into him.
He gave you hearing, and sight, and hearts;
yet little thanks do you show.

(32:4-9)

*H*ave they not seen how We drive the water
to the dry land and bring forth crops of which
they and their cattle eat?
Have they no eyes to see with?

(32:27)

*A*re they not aware of how little of the earth
and sky lies open before them,
and how much is hidden from them?
If We so willed, We could make the earth cave
in under their feet, or let fragments of the sky
fall down on them. Surely in that is a sign for
every penitent servant of Allah.

(34:9)

*S*ay: 'My Lord grants His sustenance in
abundance or gives it in scant measure to
whomsoever He will of His servants;
and whatever you spend on charity, He will pay
you back. He is the best of providers.'

(34:39)

God is He that looses the winds,
that stir up the clouds,
then We drive them on to some dead land
and therewith revive the earth, after it has died.
Such is the Resurrection.

(35:9)

The two seas are not equal; this is sweet,
delightful to taste, delicious to drink,
and that is salt, bitter to the tongue.
Yet from both you eat fresh fish, and bring forth
out of it ornaments to wear.
See how the ships plough their way through them,
as you sail away to seek His bounty.

Perchance you will be thankful.
He makes the night pass into the day and the
day into the night, and He has subjected the sun
and the moon, each of them running its course
for an appointed term.
Such is God, your Lord;
to Him belongs the Kingdom;
and the idols you invoke besides Him,
possess not so much as the skin of a date-stone.

(35:12–13)

Have you not seen how Allah sends down water out of the skies, with which We bring forth fruits of diverse colours?

And in the mountains are streaks of white and red, of various shades, and jet black rocks.

People, beasts and cattle have their different colours, too.

Even so, only those of His servants who have knowledge fear Allah; surely Allah is Almighty, All-forgiving.

(35:27–28)

God holds the heavens and the earth,
lest they fall; should they fall, none would hold
them after Him.
Surely He is All-clement, All-forgiving.

(35:41)

$\mathcal{L}$et the once-dead earth be a sign to them. We gave it life, and from it produced grain for their sustenance.

We planted it with palms and vines, and caused fountains to gush forth, so that they might feed on its fruits. It was not their hands that made all this. Will they not be thankful?

Glory be to Him, who created in pairs all the things the earth produces: the plants of the earth, human beings themselves, and living things they know nothing of.

And another sign for them is the night; We strip the day from it, and they are plunged into darkness. The sun hastens to its resting-place; its course is

ordained by the Almighty, the All-knowing.
We have determined phases for the moon
which daily wanes and in the end appears like
an aged palm-bough.
The sun is not allowed to overtake the moon,
nor does the night outstrip the day.
Each moves in its own orbit.
We gave them yet another sign when We carried
their offspring in the laden Ark.
And We have created for them similar vessels to
voyage in. If We will, We drown them, and they
have no one to cry to. No one can help or
rescue them save by Our mercy, and unless We
please to prolong their lives for a while.

(36:33-44)

*D*o they not see how, among the things Our hands have made, We have created for them the beasts of which they are the masters?
We have subjected these to them, so that they may ride on some and eat the flesh of others; they drink their milk and put them to other uses. Will they not be thankful?

(36:71-73)

*I*s humanity not aware that it was created by
Us from a sperm-drop?
Yet humans are flagrantly contentious.
People answer back with arguments
and have forgotten their own creation;
They ask, 'Who shall give back life to bones
once they are decayed?'
Say: 'He shall quicken them, who brought them
into being in the first place.
He knows all creation.
He gives you fire from the green tree
for you to kindle your fuel with.'
Is not He, who created the heavens and earth,
able to create the like of them again?
Yes indeed;
He is the All-knowing Creator.

When He decrees a thing, He need only say:
'Be,' and it is.
So glory be to Him, in whose hand
is the dominion of all things,
and to whom you shall all be recalled.

(36:77-83)

$\mathcal{I}$t was to reveal the truth that He created the heavens and the earth.

He caused the night to succeed the day, and the day to overtake the night.

He has made the sun and the moon obedient to Him,

each running for an appointed term.

Is not He the Almighty, the All-forgiving?

He created you from a single being,
then from it He created its mate;
He sent down to you eight head of cattle in pairs.
He created you in your mothers' wombs
by stages in threefold darkness.
Such then is God, your Lord;
to Him belongs the Kingdom;
there is no deity save Him.
How, then, can you turn away from Him?

(39:5-6)

$\mathcal{D}$o you not see how Allah has sent down
water out of the skies—
it penetrates the earth, and gathers in springs
beneath?
With it He brings forth crops of diverse hues.
Then they wither, and you see them turning yellow,
then He crumbles them to dust.
Surely in that is a warning for people who
understand.

(39:21)

$\mathcal{I}$t was God who made for you the night
to repose in, and the day to give you light.
God is bountiful to humanity,
yet most people are not thankful.

Such then is God, your Lord, the Creator of all
things; there is no deity save Him.
How then can you turn away from Him?
Yet even thus, they who deny the signs of God
turn away from Him.
It is God who made the earth a dwelling place
for you and heaven your canopy.
He shaped you, and shaped you well,
and provided you with good things.
Such then is God, your Lord, so blessed be God,
the Lord of the Universe.
He is the Living One;
there is no deity save Him.
So pray to Him, and worship none besides Him.
Praise be to God, the Lord of all Being.

(40:61-65)

107

It was He who created you from dust
then from a sperm-drop,
then from a blood-clot,
He brings you infants into the world
you reach adulthood then decline into old age—
(though some of you die young)
so that you may complete your appointed term
and grow in wisdom.
It is He who ordains life and death.
When He decrees a thing,
He need only say to it
'Be,' and it is.

(40:67–68)

*I*t is Allah who has provided you with the beasts, so that you may ride on some and eat the flesh of others.

You put them to many uses.

They take you where you wish to go, carrying you by land as ships carry you by sea.

And He shows you His signs; then which of Allah's signs do you reject?

(40:79-81)

Say: 'Do you disbelieve in Him who created the earth in two days, and do you claim there is any other power that could rival Him? He is the Lord of the Universe.
He set upon the earth firm mountains towering

high above its surface, and He blessed it, and in
four days, provided it with sustenance, in
accordance with differing needs.
Then He applied His design to the skies when
they were like smoke, and said to them and to
the earth,
"Come forward, willingly, or unwillingly!"
They both answered "We do come in obedience."
So He formed the sky into seven heavens
in two days,
and to each heaven He imparted its function.'
We adorned the lowest heaven with brilliant
lights and made them secure; such was the
decree of the Almighty, the All-knowing.

(41:9-12)

Among His signs are the night and the day,
the sun and moon.
Do not bow to the sun and moon.
Bow rather to Allah who created them,
if you would truly serve Him.
And if they (the pagans) wax proud, let them remember
that those who are with the Lord glorify Him
by night and day, and never grow weary.
Among His signs is the resurrection of the earth.
You see it dry and barren, but when We send
down water upon it, it quivers, and swells.
He who gives it life will raise the dead to life.
He has power over all things.

(41:37-39)

*W*e shall show them Our signs in all the regions of the earth and in their own souls, till it is evident to them

that it is the truth. Does it not suffice that your Lord is the witness of all things? Yet they still doubt that they will ever meet their Lord.

Does He not encompass all things?

(41:53–54)

Had Allah bestowed greater abundance upon His servants, they would have committed much injustice in the land.
But He sends down
in due measure whatsoever He will;
He knows and observes His servants.
It is He who sends down the rain for them after they have despaired,
and He unfolds His mercy;
He is the Protector, the All-praiseworthy.
And among His signs is the creation of the heavens and earth and the living things which He has dispersed over them;
He has the power to gather them together whenever He will.

(42:27–29)

And among His signs
are the ships that sail on the sea like mountains.
If He will, He calms the wind,
and they are becalmed on its back.
Surely in that are signs for every steadfast person
who renders thanks.
Or He causes them to founder as a punishment
for their misdeeds.
Yet He pardons much;
those who dispute Our signs shall realize they
have no escape.

(42:32–35)

*I*f you ask them, 'Who created
the heavens and earth?' they are bound to answer,
'The Almighty, the All-knowing
created them.'
It is He who has made the earth
a resting place for you, and traced out routes
upon it so that you may find your way;
who sent down out of the sky water
in due measure; and We revived thereby
a land that was dead; just in this way you too
shall be raised to life.
He created all living things in pairs,
and made for you ships

and beasts on which you ride,
so that as you mount upon their backs
you may remember your Lord's blessing
and say,
'Glory be to Him, who has subjected these to us.
But for Him, we could not be their masters.
To our Lord we shall all return.'

(43:9–14)

Surely in the heavens and earth there are
signs for the believers;
and in your own creation,
and the beasts He scatters far and near,
there are signs for true believers.
In the alternation of night and day,
and the provision Allah sends down from heaven,
with which He revives the earth after it is dead,
and in the marshalling of the winds,
there are signs for people who understand.
These are the signs of Allah that
We recite to you in truth;
But in what scripture will they believe,
if they deny Allah Himself and His signs?

(45:3-6)

$\mathcal{I}$t is Allah who has subjected to you the sea,
so that ships may sail on it at His bidding,
and so that you may seek His bounty;
and render thanks to Him.
He has subjected to you what is in the heavens
and in the earth; all is from Him.
Surely in that are signs for a people
who reflect.

(45:12-13)

$\mathcal{I}$t was to make the truth clear that
We created the heavens and the earth,
and all that lies between them;
We created them to last for an appointed term;
yet the unbelievers
give no heed to Our warning.

(46:3)

*D*o they not see that Allah
who created the heavens and earth,
not being wearied by creating them,
has the power to give life to the dead?
Yes indeed;
He has power over all things.

(46:33)

O humankind, We have created you from a
male and a female,
and made you into nations and tribes,
so that you may know one another.
Surely the noblest among you in the sight of
God is the most God-fearing of you.
God is All-knowing, and wise.

(49:13)

We know well how much the earth consumes
their bodies;
for with Us is a book recording all things.
They denied the truth whenever it was preached
to them.
So now they are in a state of confusion.
Do they not look up at the sky above them,
and mark how We have fashioned it,
and made it beautiful,
leaving no faults in its expanse?
And the earth—We spread it wide,
and set upon it firm mountains.
We caused it to bring forth every kind of
beautiful plant, thus offering a lesson and a
warning to every penitent servant.
We sent down out of heaven

blessed water,
and brought forth gardens
and the grain of harvest
and tall palm-trees laden with
clusters of dates as a provision for the servants
of God,
and We revived with it a land that was dead.
Even so shall be the Resurrection.

(50:4-11)

$\mathcal{W}$e created the heavens and the earth, and
all that lies between them, in six days, and no
sense of weariness touched Us.

(50:38)

By the dust-scattering winds
and the heavily-laden clouds; by the swiftly
gliding ships, and by the angels who deal out
blessings to all people;
that which you are promised shall be fulfilled,
and the Last Judgement shall surely come to pass!
By the heaven with its starry highways,
you contradict yourselves;
None but the perverse turn away from the true faith.

(51:1-9)

On the earth and in yourselves are signs for
firm believers.
Can you not see?
In heaven is (the source of) your provision,
and all that you are promised.
By the Lord of heaven and earth,
this is the very truth—as true as the fact that you
have the power of speech.

(51:20-23)

We built the heaven with Our might,
giving it a vast expanse, and stretched the earth
beneath.
Gracious is He who spread it out.
And all things We have made in pairs,
so that you may give thought.

(51:47-49)

$\mathcal{I}$t is the Merciful who has taught the Qur'ān.
He created humanity
and taught articulate speech.
The sun and the moon pursue their ordered course,
and the plants and the trees bow down in adoration.
And the sky—He raised it up high,
and set the Balance.
Transgress not in the Balance.
Give just weight and full measure.
And earth—He laid it out for (His) creatures,
with all its fruits, and blossom-bearing palm trees,
husked grain and scented herbs.
O which of your Lord's blessings would you deny?

(55:1-13)

We created you; then why will you not believe
in Our power?
Have you considered that seed which you spill?
Is it you yourselves who create it,
or are We the source of its creation?
We have decreed Death to be your common lot;
but there is nothing to prevent Us from
changing the nature of your existence
and creating you afresh in a fashion of which
you know nothing.
You surely know of your first creation.
So why will you not reflect?
Have you ever considered the seeds you cast on the
soil? Is it you yourselves who cause them to grow,
or are We the Cause?

If We pleased, We could turn your harvest into
chaff, so that, you would be filled with
wonderment, and exclaim 'Truly, we are ruined.
Surely we have been robbed!'
Have you ever considered the water which you drink?
Did you send it down from the clouds, or did
We send it?
If We pleased, We could make it bitter; so why
do you not give thanks?
Have you ever considered the fire which you kindle?
Did you make its timber grow, or did We?
We Ourselves made it a reminder for humanity,
and a comfort for the desert-dwellers.
Then extol the Name of your Lord,
the Almighty.

(56:57-74)

*I*ndeed, We sent Our Messengers with clear signs, and We sent down with them the Book and the scales of justice so that people might conduct themselves with fairness.

And We sent down iron, with its awsome power, and many uses for people, and so that Allah might know who helps Him, and His Messengers, in unseen.

Surely Allah is All-strong, All-mighty.

(57:25)

131

*H*e will provide for people from sources they could never imagine. Allah is All-sufficient for the person who puts his (or her) trust in Him. Allah will surely bring about what He decrees. Allah has set a measure for all things.

(65:3)

*H*e created seven heavens in harmony with
one another.
You will not see in the creation of the
All-merciful any imperfection.
Turn your gaze on it once more; can you see a
single flaw?
Yest turn your gaze again, and again, and your
gaze will fall back on you dazzled and weary.
We adorned the lowest heaven with lights,
and made them objects of futile guesses for the
evil ones;
and We have prepared for them the chastisement
of the Blazing Fire.

(67:3-5)

$\mathscr{I}$t is He who made the earth submissive to you;
therefore walk in all its regions, and eat of His
provision; to Him all shall return at the Resurrection.
Do you feel secure that He who is in heaven will
not cause the earth to cave in beneath you,
so that it will shake to pieces and overwhelm you?
Do you feel secure that He who is in heaven
will not loose against you a squall of pebbles?
You shall before long know the truth of My warning.

(67:15-17)

$\mathscr{D}$o they not see the birds above them
spreading their wings, and closing them?
Naught holds them but the All-merciful.
Surely He sees everything.

(67:19)

135

Say: 'He is the All-merciful. We believe in Him, and in Him we put all our trust. Assuredly, you will soon know who is in manifest error.'

Say: 'Consider. If in the morning all your water were to vanish into the earth,

who would bring you running water in its place?'

(67:29-30)

$\mathcal{H}$as there not been a time before man when he was not yet a thing to be thought of? We created man of a sperm-drop, intermingled in order to try him; and We gave him hearing, and sight. Surely We guided him upon the way, whether he be thankful or unthankful.

(76:1-3)

$\mathcal{B}$y the gales sent forth in swift succession; by the raging tempests and the rain-spreading winds; by your Lord's revelations, discerning good from evil and admonishing by plea and warning; that which you have been promised will be fulfilled!

(77:1-7)

$\mathcal{H}$ave We not made the earth a home for
the living and for the dead?
Have We not placed soaring mountains upon it,
and given you fresh water to drink?
Woe on that Day to the disbelievers!

(77:25-27)

$\mathcal{H}$ave We not made the earth like a cradle
and the mountains as pegs?
We created you in pairs,
and gave you rest in sleep;
and made the night a mantle,
and ordained the day for work.
We have built above you seven mighty heavens,
and placed in them a blazing lamp.
We have sent cascading down out of the rain-

139

clouds water,
So that We may bring forth grain and plants,
and luxuriant gardens.

(78:6-16)

*A*re you more difficult to create
than the heaven He built?
He raised its vault, and endowed it with order
and perfection,
giving darkness to its night,
and brightness to its day;
and the earth—after that He spread it out,
and drew water from its depth,
and brought forth its pastures.
The mountains He set firm,
for you and your cattle to delight in.

(79:27-33)

*L*et people consider their nourishment.
We poured down the rains abundantly,
then We split the earth
and brought forth grain,
grapes, reeds, olives, palms,
dense-tree'd gardens,
fruit-trees, and green pastures,
for you and your cattle to delight in.

(80:24-32)

O People! What evil has enticed you from your
gracious Lord
who created you and shaped you and wrought
you in symmetry,
and put you together in whatever form He willed?

(82:6-8)

I call to witness the sunset's fleeting afterglow,
and the night and what it encloses,
and the moon in her full perfection,
that you shall surely march onwards
from stage to stage.

(84:17-19)

M agnify the Name of your Lord the Most High
who has created and shaped all things
and proportioned them;
who has determined and guided their destinies,
who brings forth the green pasture,
then turns it to withered grass.

(87:1-5)

*W*hat, do they not consider how the camel
was created,
how heaven was lifted up,
how the mountains were firmly set,
how the earth was outstretched?
Therefore give warning!
Your duty is only to warn.
You are not charged with overseeing them.

(88:17-22)

$\mathcal{W}$e created man into a life of pain, toil and trial.
Does he think none has power over him?
He boasts, 'I have squandered enormous wealth.'
Does he think none has seen him?
Have We not given him two eyes,
a tongue, and two lips,
and guided him on the two highways?
Yet he would not attempt to ascend
the steep uphill road!
What will teach you what that steep road is?
It is the freeing of a slave,
or giving food on a day of famine
to an orphaned relation
or a needy (stranger) lying in the dust;
to have faith and to enjoin fortitude and mercy.

(90:4-17)

Consider the sun and its morning brightness
and the moon as it reflects the sun;
consider the day which reveals the world;
and the night which enshrouds it!
Consider the heaven and Him that built it,
and the earth and Him that extended it!
Consider the human soul, and Him that shaped it
and inspired it with knowledge of sin and piety.
Blessed shall be the person who causes
this (soul) to grow in purity;
and ruined the one who buries it (in darkness).

(91:1-10)

Consider the fig and the olive
and Mount Sinai
and this land secure!
We indeed created human beings in a most
noble image,
and in the end We shall reduce them to the
lowest of the low—
save those who believe, and do good works.
Theirs shall be a boundless recompense.

(95:1-6)

$\mathcal{B}$ehold, from on high We sent this down
on the Night of power;
And what could make you conceive what it is,
the Night of Power?
The Night of Power is better than a thousand
months;
on that night the angels descend in hosts bearing
divine inspiration by the leave of their Lord,
upon every command.
Peace it is, till the rising of dawn.

(97:1-5)

By the snorting chargers,
which strike fire with their hoofs as they
gallop to the raid at dawn
raising clouds of dust,
splitting apart a massed army;
Surely man is most ungrateful to his Lord!
To this he himself shall bear witness.

(100:1-7)

So that the Quraysh might remain secure,
protected in their winter and summer
journeyings:
Let them worship the Lord of this House,
who has fed them in the days of famine
and shielded them from all peril.

(106:1-4)

Select Bibliography

'Ali, Abdullah Yusuf, *The Holy Qur'an: Text, Translation, Commentary*. Washington, D.C: The Islamic Center, 1978.

'Ali, Ahmad, *Al-Qur'an: A Contemporary Translation*. New Delhi: Oxford University Press, 1987.

Arberry, Arthur, J, *The Koran Interpreted*. London: Oxford University Press, 1964.

Dawood, N.J, *The Koran, with Parallel Arabic Text*. London: Penguin Books, 1990.

Khan, Maulana Wahiduddin, *Tazkir al-Qur'an*. New Delhi: Maktaba Al-Risala, 1984.

Khan, Muhammad Muhsin, tr. *The Translation of the Meanings of Sahih Al-Bukhari. Arabic-English*. Beirut: Dar al Arabia, 1970.

Khan, Saniyasnain, *Presenting the Qur'an*. New Delhi: Goodword Press, 1997.

Kassis, Hanna, E, *A Concordance of the Qur'an*. Los Angeles: University of California Press, 1983.

Maqsood, Ruqaiyyah Waris, *The Beautiful Commands of Allah*. New Delhi: Goodword Press, 1997.

Muhammad Asad, *The Message of the Qur'an*. Gibralter: Dar al-Andalus, 1980.

Muhammad Fu'ad 'Abd al-Baqi, *al-Mu'jam al-Mufahras li Alfaz al-Qur'an al-Karim*. Cairo: Kitab al-Sha'b, n.d.

Penrice, J., *A Dictionary and Glossary of the Koran*. London: Curzon Press, 1979.

Pickthall, M.M, *The Meaning of the Glorious Koran*. New York: New American Library, 1963.

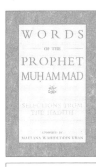

WORDS
OF THE
PROPHET
MUHAMMAD
SELECTIONS FROM
THE HADITH
COMPILED BY
MAULANA WAHIDUDDIN KHAN

INDIAN
MUSLIMS
The Need For A
Positive Outlook
Maulana Wahiduddin Khan

RELIGION
and
SCIENCE
Maulana Wahiduddin Khan

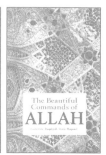

The Beautiful
Commands of
ALLAH

ISLAM
The Voice of
Human Nature
Maulana Wahiduddin Khan

WOMAN
IN ISLAMIC SHARI'AH
Maulana Wahiduddin Khan

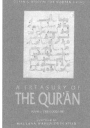

A TREASURY OF
THE QUR'AN
COMPILED BY
MAULANA WAHIDUDDIN KHAN

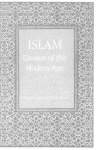

ISLAM
Creator of the
Modern Age

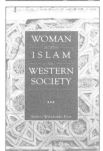

WOMAN
BETWEEN
ISLAM
AND
WESTERN
SOCIETY
Maulana Wahiduddin Khan

PRESENTING
THE QUR'AN
MAULANA WAHIDUDDIN KHAN

HIJAB
IN ISLAM
Maulana Wahiduddin Khan

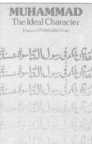

MUHAMMAD
The Ideal Character
Maulana Wahiduddin Khan

The Encyclopaedia of the Qur'an

The Encyclopaedia of the Qur'an is a unique work of reference which contains a mine of information both for family and educational use. It is extensively illustrated by photographs, maps and diagrams, many in full colour. It contains a wealth of information designed to give hours of reading, and spiritual enrichment to anyone interested in understanding the Qur'an. Ideally suited for people of all ages and backgrounds, *The Encyclopaedia of the Qur'an* is an invaluable reference book for schools and colleges, students and teachers and for professionals and scholars. Even for relaxed browsing at home, the Encyclopaedia will be found to contain a treasure trove of fascinating information affording hours of pleasurable reading. The *Encyclopaedia* is arranged in six well-illustrated sections:

1. Who's Who in the Qur'an,
2. Lands and Places of the Qur'an,
3. History of the Qur'an,
4. Understanding the Qur'an,
5. Studying the Qur'an, and
6. Dictionary of the Qur'an.

400 pages. ISBN 81-85063-86-9 (Forthcoming, 1997)
